CW00345074

797,885 Books

are available to read at

www.ForgottenBooks.com

Forgotten Books' App
Available for mobile, tablet & eReader

ISBN 978-1-330-40297-9
PIBN 10053194

This book is a reproduction of an important historical work. Forgotten Books uses
state-of-the-art technology to digitally reconstruct the work, preserving the original format
whilst repairing imperfections present in the aged copy. In rare cases, an imperfection in
the original, such as a blemish or missing page, may be replicated in our edition. We do,
however, repair the vast majority of imperfections successfully; any imperfections that
remain are intentionally left to preserve the state of such historical works.

Forgotten Books is a registered trademark of FB &c Ltd.
Copyright © 2015 FB &c Ltd.
FB &c Ltd, Dalton House, 60 Windsor Avenue, London, SW19 2RR.
Company number 08720141. Registered in England and Wales.

For support please visit www.forgottenbooks.com

1 MONTH OF
FREE
READING

at

www.ForgottenBooks.com

By purchasing this book you are eligible for one month membership to ForgottenBooks.com, giving you unlimited access to our entire collection of over 700,000 titles via our web site and mobile apps.

To claim your free month visit:

www.forgottenbooks.com/free53194

* Offer is valid for 45 days from date of purchase. Terms and conditions apply.

Similar Books Are Available from
www.forgottenbooks.com

———————◆———————

The History of Napoleon Bonaparte
by R. H. Horne

England's Battles By Sea and Land
A Complete Record, by Unknown Author

Frederick the Great and the Rise of Prussia
by W. F. Reddaway

The German Air Force in the Great War
by J. E. Gurdon

The Battle of Groton Heights
by John J. Copp

Battlefields of the World War, Western and Southern Fronts
A Study in Military Geography, by Douglas Wilson Johnson

Battles of Chattanooga, Fought Nov. 23-25, 1863, by the Armies of the Cumberland and Tennessee
by William Wehner

The Campaign of Waterloo
A Military History, by John Codman Ropes

Cawnpore
by George Trevelyan

Famous Modern Battles
by A. Hilliard Atteridge

The Fifteen Decisive Battles, of the World, from Marathon to Waterloo
by Sir Edward Creasy

Germany and the Next War
by Friedrich von Bernhardi

The History of Hyder Shah, Alias Hyder Ali Khan Bahadur, and of His Son, Tippoo Sultaun
by M. M. D. L. T.

The History of the Thirty Years' War in Germany
Translated from the German, by Frederick Schiller

History of the War in Afghanistan, Vol. 1 of 3
by John William Kaye

History of the World War
With Chronology of Important Events, by Thomas R. Best

Naval Warfare
Its Ruling Principles and Practice Historically Treated, by P. H. Colomb

Records of the Revolutionary War
by William Thomas Saffell

Why Italy Entered Into the Great War
by Luigi Carnovale

1812; The War, and Its Moral
A Canadian Chronicle, by William F. Coffin

WAR-CHRONICLE

WAR JOURNAL
SOLDIERS' LETTERS
PICTURES OF THE WAR

LIBRARY
MAY 6 1916
UNIVERSITY OF TORONTO

APRIL 1915

Printed and published by M. Berg.

The Ejection of the Russians from the Northern Point of East Prussia.

Main Head|uarters sends us the following description of the fighting on the frontier from 18th—29th March and the projected Russian attack on Tilsit:

When, towards the middle of February the Russians were obliged to make a hasty retreat from the paits of East Prussia, which they had occupied, and then after the winter battle the remnants of their X. Army were barely saved by fleeing across the Njemen and Bobr, the impressions ensuing from the fact that the Russian army had been ejected from enemy territory at all points, must have been unfavourable both in Petersburg and on the Allies. As the new X. Army was not successful in its incursions of East Prussia, and all the attacks against the southern frontiers of this province failed, the leaders hit upon the plan of taking possession of the most northern point, so as to stimulate public opinion in Russia by this "Conquest" of German territory. With this object the so-called Riga-Szawle group was formed, which mainly comprised parts of the 68th Reserve Division and frontier troops, commanded by General Apuchtin, who inaugurated an advance of his troops simultaneously towards Memel and Tilsit, about the middle of March. The Memel incidents have already been described. While the Russians there behaved like Huns, General Apuchtin's main forces appeared on 18th March, at Tauroggen, which was only occupied by 14 German Landsturm companies. The German troops were in a difficult position, opposed as they were to eight Russian battalions of the infantry regiments No. 269 and No. 270, reinforced by frontier troops and about 20 guns. Both flanks being surrounded, they had to hack their way through to Laugszargen, so as to avoid being cut off. On the left wing the Landsturm company under the leadership of Graf Hagen was in a desperate position. Although surrounded on all sides by Russians, these troops succeeded in breaking through the ring, even taking 50 Russian prisoners.

On 23rd March, the Landsturm was situated with its right wing on the Jura near Ablenken and in the neighbourhood North of this coveiing the road to Tilsit. On this day the enemy was successful in gaining possession of Ablenken. The German right wing was in imminent danger of being completely crushed and the Landsturm pushed forwaid towards the North. On this day however, the first German reinforcements arrived. They consisted of a reserve battalion from Stettin, under command of Major von der Horst, that arriving in Tilsit after a 30 hours' railway journey, drank coffee there, and then at once started off for the threatened positions. After a march of 24 kilometres the battalion arrived at Ablenken towards evening, throwing the Russians back towards the North by means of a night attack. which was splendidly carried out. In this way, the difficulties were overcome, and when during the course of the next few days further reinforcements had arrived, General von Pappritz, who was directing the operations, was able to take the offensive. The weather, which had turned to thaw, made the movements on the by-ways most difficult. The water was so high here, that on some of these roads the cannons got stuck, while the infantry waded through water, reaching to their knees, sometimes even to their waists and one artillery horse actually got drowned on the road, which had been converted into a regular bog. When the Russians recognized the measures that had been taken, they withdrew across the Jura towards Tauroggen.

Our troops that had seen or heard of some of the atrocities which the Russians had committed in Memel, filled with indescribable bitterness, pursued the enemy, who had entrenched near Tauroggen and covered the German pursuers with artillery fire from the church tower. A passage had to be erected across the Jeziorupa gorge, which entailed an amount of time, the enemy on his side taking advantage of same for increasing his fortifications and building obstacles. The first track was erected near Tauroggen farm in an icy temperature —frost had set in in the meantime—and under the most difficult conditions by the German infantry ably assisted by the pioneers. By the evening of the 28th, a bridge was ready, which was provisionally laid across the Jura, which had in the meantime begun to freeze. On 29th March, at 3 o'clock in the morning reconnoissance was finished. At this hour the assault was begun, under the leadership of Major von Nußbaum, who had already distinguished himself so brilliantly at Memel, and whose excellent battalion gave the lead for the Landwehr and Landsturm battalions. The German troops rushed across the frozen river, taking the enemy entrenchments by storm and capturing the town of Tauroggen. The Russians, seeing themselves attacked on three sides, gave up resistance after suffering heavy losses and retreated to the woods, leaving more than 500 dead and 500 prisoners, the same number of prisoners having been captured by the Germans during the preceding days. The projected Russian attack on Tilsit thus ended in success for German arms. There is not a Russian at present on German territory.

Fighting for the Meuse Heights.

Main headquarters send us the following account:

Even before Easter, it could be seen that the French would undertake fresh extensive operations against the Meuse heights occupied by the Germans, the Côtes Lorraines. The fruitlessness of a frontal attack had been experienced during the winter. On that account an attack against both flanks of the German forces between the Moselle and Meuse was inaugurated, and according to the accounts given by prisoners, a new army was formed for this.

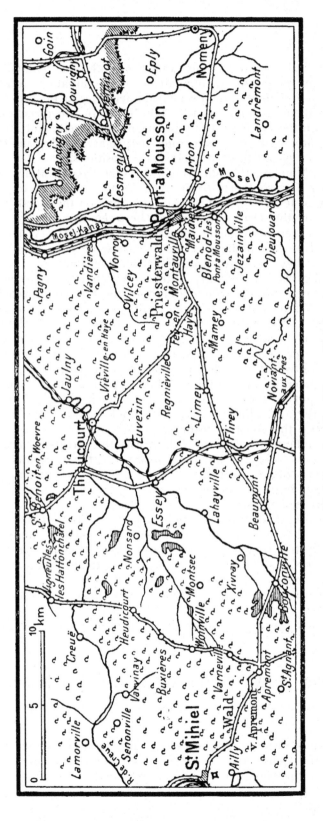

Fighting for the Meuse IIights.

After the first tentative trials and the evolutions behind the French front as observed by our airmen, the initiatory infantry fighting in Bois-le-Prêtre—the French artillery began on 3rd April to display a violent activity towards the North in the direction of Combres, and on the southern front between the Moselle and Meuse. The German outposts retired according to pre-arranged plans from Regniéville and Fey-en-Haye to their main positions.

On Easter Monday, the 5th April, the real French attack was inaugurated, on the southern front at first, to the North of Toul as well as in Bois-le-Prêtre, and at the same time on the North wing to the South of the Orne, as well as between Les Éparges and Combres. The French were not successful at any point. Wherever small troops advanced to the German trenches, or even succeeded in taking them, they were repulsed later on, everywhere.

The fighting was exceedingly bitter at two points, between the Meuse and Apremont; in the wooded territory the French approached the German positions until a destructive fire was opened upon them at short range. Especially to the East of Flirey violent fighting took place. The French rifles taking advantage of every rise or fall of ground, were followed by strong reserves, so as to proceed with the attack towards the North. The German artillery had good aim here and took every advantage of it. After a short time the reserves were put to flight, while the rifle attack collapsed under the German fire. At Flirey a bayonet attack had to be resorted to, so as to keep the German trenches.

After the infantry attack of 5th April, the artillery activity increased on both sides, with which result for the Germans, can be seen from an observation that was made on the morning of 6th April: "Hundreds of corpses were being thrown forward from the French entrenchments."

On 6th April, three more French attacks at Flirey failed. In Bois-le-Prêtre the enemy also renewed his attacks; here the 13th French infantry regiment was opposed by a Rhenish battalion with fixed bayonets, singing the "Wacht am Rhein," and before long the enemy was put to flight.

To the South of the Orne, fighting developed on 6th April which terminated successfully for us.

In the centre positions along the Meuse only artillerv duels took place.

The Fighting between the Meuse and the Moselle.

We received the following description from Main Headquarters:

I.

The report of 6th April shows that the fighting which took place between the Meuse and the Moselle, did not consist of a connected battle on the long front, which extended to a distance of almost 100 kilometres, but that at single points varying attacks were carried out by the French, and the only connecting link between the different units was the aim of surrounding the German line on two sides.

The result of the 6th of April, was that all the French attacks to the North East and East of Verdun, as well as the attacks directed against the southern wing had collapsed. A short success achieved by the French on the heights of Combres, was compensated by counter-attacks carried out by our infantry so that the heights were in German possession by evening.

The night of 6th April passed quietly after this violent fighting, in which the enemy suffered heavy casualities. But the German positions on the southern wing between Flirey and the Moselle were kept under the fire of the heavy French artillery the whole night, to which our guns successfully replied. These artillery duels lasted during the whole of the following day. Early in the morning we learned that the trenches here, were strongly reinforced by reserves, and towards 9·30 a.m. these forces began to attack, operating against Bois de Mort-Mare. Four times consecutively they assaulted our positions only to be thrown back each time with heavy losses. Heaps of dead lay before our trenches. To the East of the Bois de Mort-Mare in the open country a French attack was checked in the beginning by our artillery, while to the left in Bois-le-Prêtre it advanced as far as our positions only to collapse here under our fire.

In Bois d'Ailly the Bavarians were successful in penetrating the French positions and capturing some trenches. Latter were evacuated after having been destroyed, as their position did not prove of any tactic value to our positions.

On the northern wing the heights of Combres were under heavy artillery fire from early morning. Infantry fighting took place here again with varying success until in the afternoon all the trenches were captured by us, whereupon the French directed their fire afresh here. In the course of the afternoon the artillery fire was directed against our positions on the Woevre plains north of the heights of Combres. A vigorous and extensive French attack, which was inaugurated yesterday, completely collapsed under our fire. The day ended with German success at all points.

II.

Former reports of the fighting up to the 7th April have been given. The following days, up to the 10th, fighting continued in a lively manner. Up to April 7th, the French attacks were exclusively directed against both German wings, but the enemy is now also attacking the centre, after having assembled fresh forces in the vicinity of St. Mihiel.

Late in the afternoon of April 7th, the first attack was made from Selouse Wood, nine kilometres North of St. Mihiel, against our positions at Seuzey and La-Morville. Severe fighting took place, but the enemy was repulsed, leaving numerous dead and wounded, and losing two officers and 80 men prisoners..

During the night of April 7th—8th there were artillery actions at several points of the front, especially at the Combres height and between Regniéville and Fey-en-Haye, with infantry attacks at some points. Two attacks to the South East of Verdun near Marcheville, broke down a hundred metres before our front. At the Bois d'Ailly the French re-captured part of the trenches they had lost the day before. At daybreak, attacks on the Bois Brûlé and three night attacks on the western Bois-le-Prêtre were repulsed.

During the afternoon and night of April 8th—9th, the enemy displayed great activity at different points of the front simultaneously. An attack, which was inaugurated from the Selouse Wood, collapsed like that of the preceding day. At the same time severe fighting, which lasted for several hours, took place in the Bois de Moit-Mare in the course of which the enemy was finally driven back at the point of the bayonet, and attacks that had been undertaken in the vicinity of Regniéville, Bois-le-Prêtre, and South of the Orne, ended in the same manner.

During the night of April 8th—9th, there was a specially heavy fighting on the Combres heights. The French were apparently using fresh forces at this point. In the morning they had occupied parts of the trenches we had evacuated, owing to a severe artillery bombardment. These trenches were hotly contested during the day and we succeeded during the night of April 8th—9th in driving the enemy out of part of the trenches, while we maintained our entire main position. At daybreak, a fresh French attack with superior forces obliged us to evacuate some parts of these trenches

In consideration of these events on the Combres heights, events on the rest of the front take a secondary place, with the exception of some fires, the night of 8th—9th April passed comparatively quietly. Only at Bois de Moit-Marc, where the French had been driven back in the afternoon after bitter and long fighting, and suffering very heavy losses, they renewed their attacks in the evening without achieving any better results. But our troops that had penetrated the French position, succeeded in capturing two machine guns. In spite of this failure, the enemy decided to renew his attack early on the morning of the 9th April, which however completely collapsed.

On 9th April, the French renewed their attacks on the North wing between the Orne and the Combres heights. For instance between Parfondrupt and Marcheville, four attacks between noon and midnight, all of them on a front of six kilometres, were repulsed with severe losses. On the following night and forenoon, the French mine howitzers and artillery were active. In the afternoon, the enemy advanced on the whole line of the Combres height, having kept our positions under heavy artillery fire since the early morning.

At one point, they were successful in breaking through to the foot of the south slope before the attack broke down under the fire of our second position. Our troops maintained not only the height, but the commander of one regiment counter-attacked and thus parts of our advanced position were regained. A second French attack was stopped by effective artillery fire. During the night the enemy bombarded the height and village of Combres.

The rest of the front was opposed to an attack in the centre at the line Seuzey-Spada, which however was as unsuccessful as the others, we having made 71 prisoners. A weaker attack carried out in the Bois d'Ailly was easily repulsed and an advance across the line Regniéville-Fey-en-Haye collapsed under our artillery fire, suffering exceptionally heavy losses; 500 corpses remained lying on the ground at one point to the North of Regniéville.

On the evening of 9th April, a German attack was successful in capturing 3 blockhouses and 2 communication trenches near Croix des Carmes. 59 prisoners and 2 machine guns falling into our hands. On the 10th there were aitillery combats on the whole front. We observed the French busily throwing up new tienches and bringing up fresh troops, especially on the North wing to the South of the Orne, and in the centre opposite the position Seuzey-Spada as well as on the South wing in the neighbourhood of Regniéville. We bombaided these troops heavily and must suppose that the losses we caused were considerable, as the enemy did not attack. Near Les Eparges at the foot of the Combres height, strong French forces were bombarded by our artilleiy.

On the 10th, the sole Fiench attack on the Bois-le-Prêtre was easily repulsed. This day, like all the previous days, ended in complete German success on all the fionts attacked. On the same day the Fiench army commander, General Joffre, expressed his thanks to the I. Army for having captured the position at Les Eparges—that is the Combies height—from the Germans. Fighting has been going on for this position for weeks. and the Fiench have reported several times as to having taken and maintained these positions. The last battles for this hotly contested position have been described above. In reality the French had but occupied some tienches temporarily. All the trenches lost in these fights were recovered, with the exception of a small and unimportant portion.

III.

The days from 10th—14th April 1915, weie marked by the speciallv lively activity of the Fiench, as directed against both German wings. The 10th April passed comparatively ¡uietlv, but towards evening the enemy again displayed lively activity. Seven hundred corpses remained on the edge of the wood between the two positions after a French attack against the line Seuzey–Lamorville. Strong forces proceeded to attack also at Flirev, were, however, repulsed after having penetiated our positions at some points. In spite of that, the enemy resumed his attack early on the morning of 11th April, was again repulsed, leaving three officers and 119 men piisoners in our hands. At this point, it was obseived later that the French heaped up their dead like sand-bags on the parapets of thei entrenchments, covering them with clay. In Ailly and the western portion of Bois-le-Prêtre theie was hand to hand fighting duiing the whole night. which ended victoriously for our troops. Early on the morning of 11th Apiil. the French proceeded to attack the Combies height, which however collapsed in our artillery fire.

On 11th Apiil, fighting on both sides was limited to artilleiy duels of varying strength, now and then supported by mortai howitzers. In Bois-le-Prètre two Fiench attacks in the afternoon and evening weie diiven back at the point of the bavonet. On the Combres height the French succeeded in taking temporary possession of part of our position on the ridge, but were repulsed after bitter and violent hand to hand fighting, which lasted about two hours.

The two French attacks against our positions on the ridge of the Combres height, deserve special attention, as by means of these, the French themselves contradict the communiqué, in which General Joffre expresses his thanks to the I. Army for the final conquest of the Combres height, on 10th April. Had the French reached this goal, at which they had aimed in spite of severe losses for weeks, the above mentioned attacks on 11th April would have been not only superfluous, but a wanton and useless shedding of blood.

They were however undertaken, and repulsed by us. A French corporal, who was taken prisoner, on being questioned, related that the troops fighting at the Combres height had been told, they would only be relieved when they had taken the position, but the French Army Administration reports that no fighting took place on the Combres height since 9th April.

The night 11th—12th April passed in comparative quiet on the whole front, the stillness only being broken at certain points by unimportant artillery and infantry attacks.

On 12th April, only artillery fire was to be reported along the whole front, from the Combres height as far as Richecourt, but a very heavy shelling of our positions on the North wing, between Buzy and Marcheville, as well as on the South wing in the section to the East of Richecourt gave signs that infantry attacks were to be expected. These were inaugurated simultaneously, operating in the vicinity of Maizeray and Marcheville. While the enemy refrained from repeating his attack at last mentioned place, at Maizeray where after the first attack all the participators had remained lying on the ground, he repeated it by making two further attempts, an hour intervening between each. the attacking troops were thereby totally annihilated, one officer and 40 men only having been taken prisoners. Notwithstanding these losses, the French attacked once more, late in the evening near Marcheville with three consecutive lines supported by massed columns, but our artillery put a speedy end to this fifth attack, in which two armoured motors were employed. At the same time an infantry attack was repulsed on the South wing to the West of Bois-le-Prêtre. It was observed here, that coloured troops were employed in throwing up trenches.

After a comparatively quiet night, infantry fighting began again on both wings on the morning of the 13th April. This time, the French advanced on our position at Maizeray and Marcheville without an artillery display, but if they had expected to surprise our troops, they were disappointed and the attack driven back easily. Fighting was continued in Bois-le-Prêtre, and to the North of Maizeray the enemy attempted anew to penetrate our positions, this like the former attacks, being driven back.

On the night of 13th April, the French kept up a violent infantry fire on the North wing, supported now and then by heavy artillery, so as to prevent repairs being carried out in our positions. An attack, which took place early in the morning, collapsed before our lines, the same fate overtaking the infantry attacks to the North of Marcheville, which were undertaken in the course of the day. On a narrow front, the enemy advanced on our position three times, at each new attempt fresh forces being brought up to stem the retreating troops and continue the attack.

According to the recitals of prisoners, the infantry regiment No. 51 was decimated. In Bois d'Ailly three infantry attacks were preceded by blasting, which was not very effective and all three were repulsed. To the North of Flirey, the French had a small success, where they took possession of a trench about 100 metres deep. The violent hand to hand fighting lasted during the whole day and had not been decided when evening fell. To the West of Bois-le-Prêtre near fighting took place also, which finished in the evening with the defeat of the enemy, who suffered exceptionally heavy losses. On the rest of the front, artillery fighting was reported on 14th April, with varying success, and at some points near fighting was in progress. A French officer, who has been taken prisoner, reported that the enemy artillery has unlimited supplies of American ammunition.

Already on 12th April, strong forces were noticed crossing the Meuse in an eastern direction to the North of St. Mihiel. This in conjunction with the remarkably great activity, displayed by the French airmen, is a sign that the fighting between the Meuse and the Moselle has not yet reached its end.

IV.

The cessation of the French operations between the Meuse and Moselle, after the preceding attacks, which had ended so disastrously for them, could be noticed towards the end of the second week of April, and has continued since 14th April, the date of our last report, until to-day, the 19th. There is quiet along the whole front, but by quiet must be understood a lack of important combined offensive operations—and not a cessation of all fighting activity. The noise of the cannons does not die altogether either by day or night; at some points even, the heavy artillery fire is increased with great violence. The near fighting accessories—mine howitzers, hand grenades, and trench mines—are employed, and the infantry and machine gun fire never cease altogether. Both opponents try to render the streets and quarters behind the fronts unsafe by means of artillery fire and aviators bombs. The lively activity displayed by marching troops, as well as an increase in the railway and motor traffic behind the French lines, especially on 15th and 16th April, shows that the present conditions of comparative quiet can hardly be expected to last.

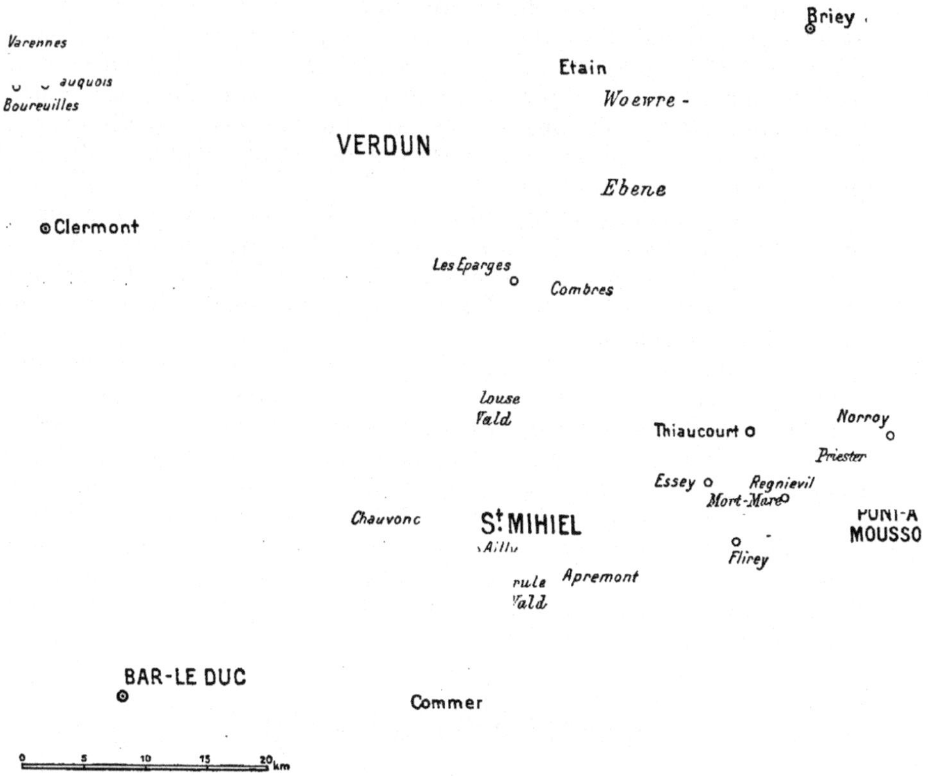

Briey

Varennes

Etain

auquois

Woewre -

Boureuilles

VERDUN

Ebene

◎Clermont

Les Eparges

Combres

louse
Vald

Norroy

Thiaucourt ○

Priester

Essey ○   Regnievil
Mort-Mare○

Chauvonc   St MIHIEL

PUNT-A
MOUSSO

Ailly

○ ·
Flirey

rule   Apremont
Vald

BAR-LE DUC
◎

Commer

0   5   10   15   20 km

The days from 14th—19th April, were principally marked by
artillery duels, while the French infantry, probably still suffering
from the impressions of losses sustained in the foregoing battles,
limited itself to isolated attacks, which were repulsed without
exception, and of no importance when the whole situation is taken
into account. These attacks were repeated almost exclusively in
the sections of our front, against which, since the beginning of the
fighting the French offensive has been specially directed, on the
North wing against our positions at Marcheville–Maizeray and
Combres, and on the South wing against our lines in the Bois
d'Ailly, Bois Mort-Mare, to the North of Regniéville, Fey-en-Haye,
and in the Bois-le-Prètre.

On the night of 14th—15th April, the attacks on the Combres
height were especially violent. The enemy here employed fumes
and obnoxiously smelling bombs, which spread a haze of smoke
and poisonous gasses before and around our positions, so as to
prevent a view of the enemy and increase the difficulties of our
troops in the trenches.

14

An advance in Bois-le-Prêtre, undertaken by our troops the same night, ended with the capture of a part of the French main position, which juts out here with a strongly fortified *point d'appui* against our foremost trenches. The hand to hand fighting, which was inaugurated with this success in the western Bois-le-Prêtre, lasted the following days and nights without interruption. We are progressing slowly but surely.

On the morning of the 19th, our troops here were successful in blowing up two blockhouses and the adjoining trenches, which enabled us to advance our position. The French sustained considerable losses here, while we did not lose one single man in spite of the success gained.

The 15th April brought two French attacks in Bois d'Ailly, both of which—the second when only in preparation—collapsed in our fire. In the same way two advances undertaken by the enemy to the North of Flirey on the night of 16th April, were repulsed. During these days we noticed repeatedly at different points, for instance at the Combres height, at Flirey, and opposite the wood Mort-Mare, that the French troops in the foremost trenches were standing by, but no attacks took place. Artillery activity on both sides during the space from 14th—19th April was really all that could be reported.

General Dubail's "Wedge."

Main Headquarters writes the following:

How the French officers try with all possible means to spur on their men to advance, is proved by the following command, issued by General Dubail, leader of the I. French Army, and dated 5th April 1915.

For the past three months, the German Army Corps between the Meuse and the Moselle have suffered so much on account of their numerous and energetic attacks, that their resistance has now been considerably lessened. Several regiments have had to be relieved recently. Some were withdrawn on account of the losses that we have inflicted, or have changed their section (for instance the Bavarian Regiments of the 33rd Division, which were almost annihilated near Les Eparges). The others were transported to other points of the theatre of war, to support the lines that had become thin in some places. One regiment of the V. Army Corps was taken to Belgium and two regiments belonging to the same Corps, have been sent against Russia. The heavy artillery, which three months ago was so amply provided with ammunition, has decreased and is less active.

So as to oppose our attacks, which were carried out recently on the line Fey-en-Haye, Bois-le-Prêtre, the Germans were obliged to bring up reserves from their adjoining sections, and it appears that these latter are not available in very considerable numbers.

On 30th March, we succeeded in capturing the German positions at Bois-le-Prétre and before Fey-en-Haye in a breadth of 1,000 metres and a depth of 800 metres. On 31st March, Fey-en-Haye itself was taken, and on 3rd April, the positions at Regniéville. On a front of 40 kilometres the I. Army which had been reinforced prepared storm positions.

To-morrow we shall close the pincers, within which we have enclosed the enemy between Verdun and Pont-à-Mousson, and carry out frontal and rear attacks with considerable forces, thus destroying the enemy troops situated between Metz and St. Mihiel.

Every soldier must be aware of the following fact: The cannons which he hears in front of him, are French guns that are firing on the enemy's rear.

At present the Germans seem only to be able to bring up local reserves to ward off this dreadful attack, and even if they have others, there can only be a question of some battalions.

Signed: Dubail.

Between the Meuse and Moselle.

Incorrectness of the French Official Communiqué.

Main Headquarters writes the following:—

9th April 1915.

The French Communiqué (Eiffelturm) of 9th April 1915 (afternoon) enumerates in a resumé the alleged successes achieved by the French troops in the fighting between the Meuse and the Moselle. This French description deserves closer attention, as the fertile imagination of the author of these reports reaches an extraordinary height in this. Each of the four statements, contained in the resumé, shall therefore be considered separately.

1. The heights situated to the West of the Orne and commanding this river as well as the villages of Gussainville and Fromezey were never in the hands of the Germans. The French attacks inaugurated against the German position from these points collapsed without exception under our artillery fire and retired with heavy losses. This unsuccessful advance from the above named line, which had never been held by us, the French seem consider as conquest.

2. The word "almost" with which the report limits the French success on the heights at Les Eparges, deserves special attention. In reality, the French do not hold any position on the heights, although they succeeded in penetrating some trenches on the northern slope under the ridge.

3. As in the first mentioned case, the French consider as a conquest the possession of places never held by the Germans. We never even attempted to gain this territory. The fighting during the last weeks took place in the Bois d'Ailly itself, where small

parts of the German intrenchments were temporarily in the hands of the French.

4. In the villages, lying in front of our fighting line, Regniéville and Fey-en-Haye, we had only advanced "listening posts" which retired, according to pre-arranged plans, on the French attack. As at this part of the fighting line the intrenchments of both armies are only separated by a space varying from 100—500 metres and as we have not lost anything, it is a mathematical impossibility for the French to have gained a strip of 3 kilometres.

Shells containing poisonous gas.

Main Headquarters send the following:—

22nd April 1915.

In a publication dated 21st inst., the English Army Administration complains that on the recapture of "Hill 60" South East of Ypres, the Germans "contrary to all rules of civilized warfare" employed shells, which exploded poisonous. asphyxiating gases. As can be seen by the German official reports, our enemies have been making use of these for months; but they appear to be of opinion that what is permissible for them, is not permissible for us. Such an opinion, which is nothing new in this war, we can understand—especially when we consider that owing to the development of German chemistry we are in a position to employ more effective means than our enemies,—we can understand this although we do not share it. Besides the reference to the rules of warfare does not hold good.

The German troops do not employ any "shells, the sole object of which is spreading obnoxious or poisonous gases" (Declaration at Hague 29th July 1899), and the gases developed by the German shells, although not so dangerous as the French, Russian, and English artillery shells, are very much more disagreeable. The asphyxiating fumes employed by us in hand to hand fighting, are not in any way contradictory to the "Laws of Warfare." They do not produce anything more than the powerful effects, which could be achieved by kindling a bundle of straw or dry wood. As the smoke thus produced can be clearly seen, even on a dark night, everyone is at liberty to withdraw from its effects in good time.

The Treatment of the captured Crews of the German Submarines.
German and American Notes.

The North German Gazette (Norddeutsche Allgemeine Zeitung) publishes the following Notes, referring to the treatment of the captured crews of German submarines:

Note sent by the German Foreign Office, to the Embassy of the U. S. A. in Berlin.
(Translation.)

According to notices appearing in the British press, the British Admiralty is said to have made known its intention not to accord to officers and crews of German submarines, who have become prisoners, the treatment due to them as prisoners of war, especially not to concede to the officers the advantage of their rank.

The German Government is of the opinion that these reports are not correct, as the crews of the submarines acted in the execution of orders given to them, and in doing this, have solely fulfilled their military duties. At any rate, the reports in question have become so numerous in the neutral press, that an immediate explanation of the true facts appears to be of most urgent importance. if for no other reasons than consideration of public opinion in Germany.

The Imperial Foreign Office therefore requests the American Embassy to have inquiry of the British Government made by telegraph, through the medium of the American Embassy in London, as to whether and in what way they intend to treat officers and crews of German submarine boats, who have been made prisoners, in any respect worse than other prisoners of war.

Should this prove to be the case, the request is added that in the name of the German Government sharpest protest be lodged with the British Government against such proceedings and that no doubt be left that for each member of the crew of a submarine made prisoner, a British army officer held prisoner of war in Germany, will receive corresponding harsher treatment. The Imperial Foreign Office would be grateful for information at the earliest convenience regarding the result of the steps taken.

The Note handed to the German Imperial Foreign Office by the American Embassy in Berlin.

Berlin, 6th April 1915.

Note verbale.

With reference to the estimated Note verbale $\frac{\text{No. III b 6,755}}{34,557}$ of March 16th, 1915, regarding the treatment of the crews of German submarines who have become prisoners in England, the American Embassy has the honor to inform the Imperial Foreign Office that the matter was at once brought to the attention of the Department of State at Washington and begs to quote herewith to the Imperial Foreign Office the reply of the British Government in the matter, which has been received telegraphically from Washington:

"The Secretary of State for Foreign Affairs presents his compliments to the United State's Ambassador, and with reference to his Excellency's Note of 20th ultimo, respecting reports in the press

E

upon the treatment of prisoners from German submarines, has the
honour to state that he learns from the Lords Commissioners of
the Admiralty, that the officers and men, who were rescued from
the German submarines "U 8" and "U 12" have been placed in
the Naval Detention Barracks, in view of the necessity of their se-
gregation from other prisoners of war.

In these quarters they are treated with humanity, given oppor-
tunities for exercise, provided with German books, subjected to no
forced labour, and are better fed and clothed than British prisoners
of equal rank now in Germany.

As, however, the crews of the two German submarines in
question, before they were rescued from the sea, were engaged in
sinking innocent British and neutral merchant ships, and wantonly
killing non-combatants, they cannot be regarded as honourable opponents, but rather as persons who, at the orders of their Government, have committed acts, which are offences against the law of
nations and contrary to common humanity.

His Majesty's Government would also bring to the notice of
the United State's Government that during the present war more
than 1,000 officers and men of the German Navy have been rescued
from the sea, sometimes in spite of danger to the rescuers, and
sometimes to the prejudice of British naval operations. No case
has, however, occurred of any officer or man of the Royal Navy
being rescued by the Germans."

Reprisals on Prisoners.
Text of German Note to United States' Ambassador in Berlin.

Berlin, 11th April 1915.

The undersigned has the honour of communicating the following to His Excellency, the Ambassador of the United States of
America, Mr. James W. Gerard, in answer to the Verbal Note of
6th inst.—F. O. No. 2928—regarding the treatment of the crews of
German submarines prisoners in England:

"The German Government has learned with astonishment and
indignation that the British Government regards the officers and
crews of German submarines not as honourable enemies, and ac-
cordingly treats them not as other prisoners of war, but as ordi-
nary prisoners (Arrestanten). These officers and crews acted as
brave men in the discharge of their military duties, and they are
therefore fully entitled to be treated like other prisoners of war, in
accordance with international arrangements. The German Government therefore enters the strongest protest against a procedure,
which is contrary to international law, and sees itself at the same
time regretfully compelled immediately to execute the reprisals announced by it and subject to similar harsh treatment, a corresponding number of English army officers, who are prisoners of war.

When, moreover, the British Government sees fit to remark that the German Navy, in contrast to the British, failed to save shipwrecked men, we can only reject with loathing the insinuation that such rescue was possible for German ships, but was wilfully neglected by them.

The undersigned begs the Ambassador to convey this information to the British Government, and also to take steps for securing a member of the American Embassy in London an opportunity of personally enquiring into the treatment of German submarine prisoners and present a report concerning the details of their lodging, maintenance, and employment. Further proceedings with regard to British officers, who have been provisionally placed under officers' arrest (Offiziershaft) will depend upon treatment of the German prisoners.

The undersigned expresses his thanks to the Ambassador for his kind interference in this disagreeable matter.

v. Jagow.

Contradiction of British Calumnies concerning the German Navy.

Berlin, April 15, 1915.

In the interchange of notes concerning the treatment of our submarine crews, Prisoners of War in England, the British Government refers to the fact, that during the present war more than a thousand officers and men of the German Navy have been rescued from the Sea by British War Ships, while no officer or man of the British Navy has been rescued by the Germans.

In answer to this, the following has been ascertained on reliable authority:

In cases, in which British War Ships were sunk by German submarines, rescuing the crew is out of the question, as submarines are not in a position to give such assistance.

In the naval battle off Helgoland on August 28, 1914, and the raids on the English coast on November 2, and December 16, 1914, torpedo boats were destroyed, but the British Government can hardly refer to these cases, as it disputes the loss of all vessels.

In the fighting off the Doggerbank on January 24, 1915, the English battle cruiser "Tiger" and a number of English torpedo boats were lost, but in this case again the British Government has officially declared that all ships taking part in the fighting, had returned.

On September 20, 1914, the English cruiser "Pegasus" was destroyed in the English port of Zanzibar by the small cruiser "Königsberg." The "Königsberg" was outside the harbour and could not be expected to run into an enemy harbour, so as to rescue the crew. Thus only remains the battle off Coronel, in the course of which two English armoured cruisers were destroyed by our squadron on November 1, 1914.

Our ships lost sight of the "Good Hope" on darkness falling, they looked for her, but without success and did not even know whether she had been sunk or not. It can thus clearly be seen that none of the "Good Hope's crew" could be saved. When the "Monmouth" was sunk, H. M. S. "Nürnberg" was the only vessel near, and a letter, which Graf Spee's son has written, shows why nobody could be saved, as the extract from his letter will show:

"The 'Monmouth' sank with her flag flying and we could not save any of the crew. First, on account of the heavy sea, which made it impossible to lower our boats and then because fresh smoke had been reported, which we hoped was bringing us some more enemies towards whom we steamed."

The commander of the squadron, Graf Spee, referring to this in a letter, mentions:

"Unfortunately the work of rescue was made impossible by the heavy sea."

In Germany it has been universally admitted that English war ships rescued our men after battles. But it never occurred to anyone in Germany to reproachfully recall the fact, that at the battle of the Falklands, when our "Scharnhorst" sank with her flag flying in broad daylight and a smooth sea, that none of the crew was saved, although numerous British ships were in the vicinity.

From the above it can clearly be seen that during the whole course of the war, German war ships never had an opportunity of rescuing the crews of British war ships. The British Government knows this quite as well as we do, but it refrains from saying so in its Note, and by comparing the facts that the British Navy has rescued more than a thousand German seamen, while the German Navy has not saved a single British sailor, tries to accuse the German Navy of having intentionally refrained from rescuing the men. Here we have another proof of the cunning means employed for deceiving public opinion and inciting the neutrals against Germany. The German Note repudiates with horror, the accusations contained in the British Note.

War Journal

April 1.

Bismarck's centenary celebrated. The Kaiser issues a proclamation in honour of the Chancellor.

The German East Army's war booty for the month of March amounted to 55,800 Russian prisoners, 9 cannons, 61 machine guns.

The steamer "Emma" from Le Havre torpedoed and sunk by a submarine.

Newspaper representatives ejected from Tenedos by the English.

A number of native Indian authorities relieved of their posts; cessation of transports to Europe by the Viceroy.

April 2.

In and around Bois-le-Prêtre, fighting continues. We inflicted several severe losses on the enemy, driving him back to his former positions.

The English steamer "Seven Seas" and three fishing boats sunk, as well as the Norwegian barque "Nor" by German submarines.

Between Pruth and the Dnjestr a strong Russian attack repulsed, the Russians suffering heavy losses.

An attempt at landing made by the English near Mouaileh on the coast of Hedschas thwarted.

April 3.

Arrival of the American Note in London.

Russian troops landed in the Persian province of Enseli.

April 4.

Our troops captured Drie Grachten from the Belgians, on the West Bank of the Yser Canal.

In the Carpathians, fighting continues to both sides of the Laborcza valley; to the East of Viravas, strong Russian attacks repulsed. 2,020 Russians taken prisoners.

Two Russian ships "Provident" and "Vastochnaja" sunk by the Turks near Odessa.

E

The Turkish cruiser "Medjidje" struck a mine while following the mine sweepers. The crew was saved.

From the submarine war. The English steamer "Olvine" torpedoed between Guernsey and Calais, also the Russian sailing boat "Hermes" off the Isle of Wight.

April 5.

French attacks in the Argonnes repulsed by our artillery and at Boureuilles driven back before our obstacles. as well as at Pont-à-Mousson. We gained ground at Bois-le-Prêtre owing to mines.

A Russian attack at Mariampol repulsed, the enemy suffering heavy losses.

Fighting in the Laborcza valley continued.

Strong hostile forces aimed at the southern bank of the Dnjestr repulsed at Uscie Biskupie. 1,400 prisoners and 7 machine guns captured.

April 6.

Strong attacks carried out by the French between the Meuse and the Moselle in the vicinity of Verdun, Ailly, Apremont, Flirey and Pont-à-Mousson, were repulsed, the enemy suffering heavy losses. It is to be expected that attacks here will be continued, as the enemy has begun to realize the fruitlessness of his efforts in the Champagne.

Russian attacks repulsed to the South of Kalwarja and to the East of Augustow—the situation in the East is otherwise unchanged.

Austrian and German troops took strong Russian positions on the heights to the East of Laborcza valley in the Carpathians, taking 5,040 prisoners, and later on further batches amounting to 2,530 men were captured.

To the North East of Ottynias (South Eastern Galicia) a Russian night attack repulsed.

From the submarine war. The English collier "City of Bremen torpedoed off Landsend, the English steamer "Northland" torpedoed off Beachy Head.

April 7.

Drie Grachten evacuated by our troops owing to the English and French heavy artillery; to the East and South East of Verdun, French attacks were thwarted, the enemy suffering very heavy casualities.

The enemy was thrown back to his former position at Ailly, owing to a counter-attack carried out by our troops.

Vice-admiral Sonchon commanding the Turkish fleet.

The Kaiser among his officers and men distributing decorations at the French theatre of war

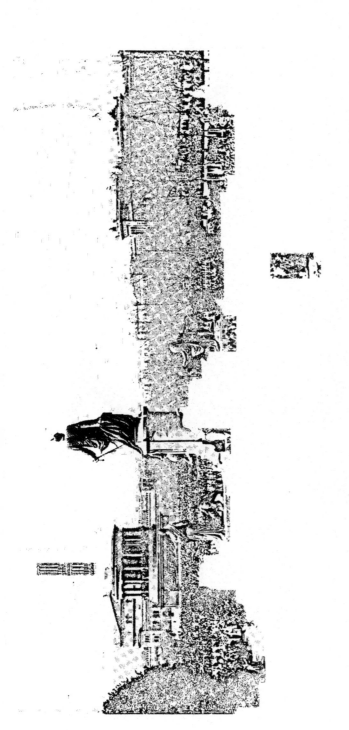

B smarck s cen enary: The ce ebration ook place at the Bismarck monument before he Re chs ag building n Berlin on 1st April 19¹5.

Feldmarshal General von Hindenburg, Comm ander-in-chief of the Eas ern A my nspecting a mo o s edge.

The wellknown Swedish nqurer and author, Sven Hedin, watching a battle on the eastern heatre of war n Po and. Sven Hedin s he second figure from he left on he picture.

New y equipped nfantry on the po n t of marching out in he ene ny country.

German Guards marching to the line of battle: The newly equipped regimen leaves the barracks to the strains of martial music.

400 captured Russian field guns, in the background 107 Fr

400 captured French and Engl

rtress guns of various calibre at the Krupp works in Essen.

ıs at the Krupp works in Essen.

A new German acquisition: A bath train for German soldiers. The first wagon contains 0 showers and one bath for officers. In the wo following wagons there are 16 showers, which can be used by office s and men on he journey o the fron and from thence home.

One o the German pioneers' mas erpieces: A railway br dge tha was cons ruc ed n one day.

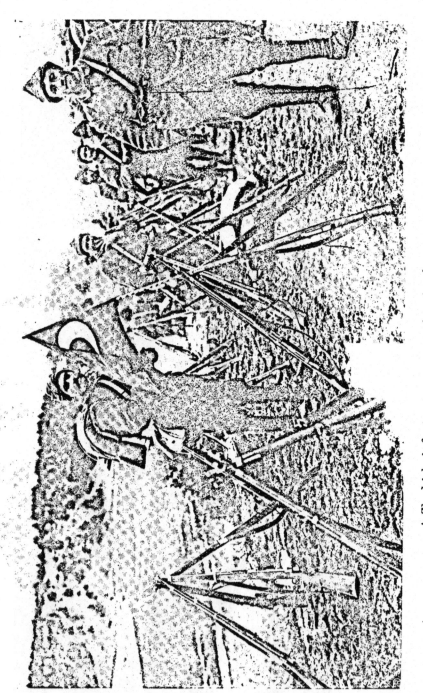

A Turkish infantry co umn resting in the mountains.

Mohammedan prisoners in the camp at Zossen.

Choral Society (Gesangverein) of French prisoners at Zossen.

The German prisoners' camp in Gubin. Distribution of underlinen to the Russian prisoners.

Advancing in Russian territory in the direction of Andrzejewo, South East of Memel, we destroyed a Russian battalion, repulsing another; our losses amounted to six killed. The booty captured in the fighting that took place at the Laborcza valley has increased by 930 prisoners, 2 cannon, 7 machine guns, and 5,000 rifles.

We bombarded Belgrade as a reprisal for the shelling of the open town of Orsova (on the Danube).

From the submarine war. It is reported that "U 29" with commander Otto Weddigen and crew has been lost.

April 8.

The fighting between the Meuse and Moselle continues. French attacks on the Woevre plains were unavailing, as well as to the North of St. Mihiel and Flirey and advances in Bois-le-Prêtre. The enemy suffered enormous losses in the course of these attacks.

Fighting continues for the Hartmannsweilerkopf.

The incessant Russian attacks to both sides of the Laborcza valley repulsed by our Allies. The number of the Russian unwounded prisoners taken in the "Easter battles in the Carpathians" amounts to 10,000.

According to a Reuter report, the commander of the auxiliary cruiser "Prinz Eitel Friedrich" has requested the American authorities to intern his ship, owing to the non-arrival of expected assistance.

April 9.

The Belgians again driven out of Drie Grachten; two enemy officers, a hundred men, and two machine guns captured.

Reims subjected to howitzer grenades as a reprisal for the French shelling of places behind our front.

In the fighting which continues between the Meuse and Moselle, the enemy suffered heavy casualities in the course of fruitless attacks. Progress continues in the Bois d'Ailly.

In the wooded regions of the Carpathians, the continuous frontal attacks carried out by the Russians, collapse, the enemy suffering heavy losses.

According to an official communication, it is estimated that 812,808 enemies are in the hands of the Germans.

April 10.

The booty of Drie Grachten has been increased to 5 Belgian officers, 122 men, and 5 machine guns.

The French suffered a heavy defeat between the Orne and the heights of the Meuse (on 9th).

On the western side of the Bois-le-Prêtre. the enemy lost that part of the position to which he had advanced the end of March.

The Russian attacks at Kalwarja repulsed with heavy losses; the situation in the East is otherwise unchanged.

From the submarine war. The Portuguese sailing vessel "Douro" with the cargo of coals from Cardiff to Oporto, torpedoed by a German submarine, the crew rescued and landed in Swansea.

The French sailing ship "Chateaubriand" torpedoed by a German submarine. The English steamer "Harpalyce" destroyed either by a submarine or mine.

April 11.

It has been ascertained that the French sustained very severe losses in the fighting between the Meuse and the Moselle.

A fresh attack directed against the Combres height fails.

A German Note to America, protesting against the non-maintenance of strict neutrality.

The English steamer "Southpoint" torpedoed by "U 28" off Cape Finisterre.

April 12.

39 English officers, prisoners of war, removed to Military Detention Barracks (Militär-Arrestanstalten) as a reprisal for the refusal by the English Government to treat the prisoner crews of our submarines with the honour due to their rank.

Bombs dropped on Nancy as reprisal for the French bombs dropped on Müllheim (Baden).

1,350 Russians captured to the East of Mariampol. Cessation of Russian attacks in the Carpathians.

From the submarine war. The English steamer "Wayfarer" torpedoed and towed to Queenstown.

The "Kronprinz Wilhelm" ran into the harbour of Newport News.

April 13.

Renewed French attacks at Maizeray and Marcheville between the Meuse and Moselle collapsed.

Russian attempts to advance at the Uzsok Pass repulsed.

From the submarine war. A French threemaster sunk, the English steamer "President" and a French steamer "Frédéric Frank" damaged by a German submarine.

Agadir occupied by Mussulmen.

April 14.

Recapture of the Czeremcha heights at the Uzsok Pass by two Hungarian infantry regiments.

Riots spread in India in the provinces of Lahore, Delhi, and Bengal.

April 15.

The French attacked three times at Marcheville without success.
An enemy airman dropped bombs on Freiburg i. B.
A Zeppelin made a raid on the mouth of the Tyne.
The Austrians stormed an important height near Wysockowz.
From the submarine war. The English steamer "Armigan" torpedoed.
Proclamation of the "Holy War" by the Emir, mobilization measures in Afghanistan.

April 16.

French airmen made an attack on Rottweil and Haltingen (Baden).
German naval airships made a successful raid on fortified places on the English South coast.
One of the enemy armoured cruisers leaves the Dardanelles for Tenedos, after having been damaged by the Turks.
Tsingtau declared to be a second continental harbour for the Japanese fleet.
Newspaper reports as to the landing of 4,000 Japanese in Turtlebay on Mexican territory.

April 17.

An enemy airship drops 12 bombs on Straßburg.
A French position to the North West of Perthes (Champagne) stormed.
The captain of the "Thordis" decorated by the King and English Government for having rammed a German submarine.
England offers a full apology to the Chilean Government on account of the "Glasgow" and "Dresden" incident.
Occupation of Casablanca by Morocco Mussulmen.
Occupation of Schakalskoppe, Kuibes, Bethaney, and Brackwasser by troops of the South African Union.
German airmen over Calais, Amiens, Sainte-Menehould, Nancy, Pont-à-Mousson, Lunéville.

The English submarine "E 15" sunk in the Dardanelles to the East of Karanlik Liman.

The English defeated at Jassini on 19th January, by our German East African troops.

The Island of Mafia occupied bv the English on 10th and 11th January

April 18.

The Greek steamer "Hellespontos" bound for Montevideo fiom Ymuiden, sunk in the North Sea.

At Nagypolony, Zellö and Telepocz in the Carpathians 1,425 Russians and 7 officers taken prisoners.

April 19.

German airmen dropped bombs on Warsaw.

A Turkish torpedo boat that had attacked the English transport ship "Manitou," grounded on the coast of Chios and was blown up by its crew. 24 men from the "Manitou" drowned and 27 missing.

Von der Goltz Pascha made Commander-in-General of the 1. Turkish Army.

Proclamation of conditions of war in Tunis and Algeria.

The American cruiser "New Orleans" sent to examine into affairs in Turtlebay.

April 20.

Our troops penetrated the French main position at Croix des Carmes.

French airmen dropped bombs on Kandern and Lörrach (Baden).

Russian airmen dropped bombs on Insterburg.

The English fishing trawler "Vanilla" sunk by a German submarine.

Seeheim and Keetmannshoop occupied by troops of the South African Union.

April 21.

French attacks at Flirey, Metzeral and Sondernach repulsed.

German airmen drop bombs on Amiens and Bialystok.

Renewed air-attacks attempted by the French on Lörrach.

A British submarine sunk in the German Bight (North Sea) in cause of an attack on several submarines.

4,000 Indians attacked English troops at Schabkads on 18th April.

April 22.

Secretary of State Bryan in answer to a memorandum sent by the German Ambassador Graf Bernstorff stated that an embargo on ammunition on the part of the United States of America would be a violation of neutrality.

The British Admiralty issues an official proclamation stating that shipping between Holland and England will be temporarily suspended.

April 23.

Our troops effected a crossing of the Yser Canal at Steenstraate. Langemarck, Steenstraate, Het Sas and Pilkem captured.

The German fleet cruising in the North Sea, advanced as far as English waters without meeting any British naval forces.

The Landungskoıps of the "Emden" ("Ayesha" crew) arrived in Lidd on 27th March, having suffered severe losses owing to an attack, which a hand of Arabs, bribed by the English, had carried out.

April 24.

Lizerne, West of the Ypres Canal, stormed. English and French attacks at Ypres are thwarted. 2,470 prisoners, 35 guns, and numerous machine guns captured.

Renewed French attacks between the Meuse and the Moselle.

State Secretary von Tirpitz celebrates his 50th anniversary in State Service.

The English fishing trawler "Saint Lawrence" and the Russian steamer "Frack" sunk by German submaıines.

April 25.

Further success reported from Ypres. The farm Solaert as well as St. Julien and Kersselaere taken by storm. Victorious advance towards Grafenstafel. 1,000 English taken prisoners and several machine guns captured. Enemy counter-attacks repulsed with heavy losses.

On the heights of the Meuse to the South-West of Combres, the French suffered a heavy defeat. 24 enemy officers, 1,600 men, and 17 guns captured.

Fresh success achieved by our Allies in the Orawa valley. The Ostry height taken by assault.

From the air war. 29 bombs were dropped on the railway point Bialystok, as a reprisal for the Russian bombs dropped on Neidenburg.

From the submarine war. Reuter reports that three British fishing trawlers were sunk by our submarines.

April 26.

Fighting continues at Ypres. The number of the captured guns has increased to 45, inclusive the 4 heavy English ones. The entire number of prisoners amounts to 5,000.

In the Champagne to the North of Beau Séjour, French night attacks were repulsed. On the Meuse heights several hills taken by assault—in the Vosges, the Hartmannsweilerkopf recaptured. 11 officers, 749 men, 6 mine throwers, and 4 machine guns captured.

In the Carpathians, the Russians forced to make a hasty retreat at the Uzsok Pass. On the pursuit carried out by our Allied 26 trenches occupied and a quantity of war booty captured.

Enemy attacks at the Dardanelles by water and land repulsed (on 25th).

April 27.

Violent English attacks directed against our new lines in Flandeis collapsed under our fire, the enemy suffering exceptionally heavy losses.

Continued progress on the Meuse Heights—all enemy attacks against the Hartmannsweilerkopf failed.

At the Dardanelles, the enemy's attempts to land troops at the mouth of the Sighindere and in the coast district to the West of Kaba Tepe were completely forced back by Turkish troops, the enemy suffering very heavy losses.

From the submarine war. The French armoured cruiser "Leon Gambetta" torpedoed at night by an Austrian submarine. Part of the crew rescued by Italian ships. Another fishing boat torpedoed in the North Sea by a German submarine.

April 28.

We succeeded in maintaining our new positions in Flandeis in spite of renewed enemy attacks, which collapsed in our fire.

In the Champagne, a considerable group of French fortifications to the North of Le Mesnil, captured and consolidated. 60 uninjured French, 4 machine guns, and 13 mine throwers captured.

To the North-East and East of Suwalki, we captured Russian positions on a front of 20 kilometres.

At the Dardanelles renewed enemy attempts against Kaba Tepe and to the South Coast of Gallipoli repulsed.

In the Caucasus, Russian night attacks directed against Turkish outposts to the North of Milo repulsed.

April 29.

Enemy attacks on our positions at Steenstraate and Het Sas as well as on our right wing to the East of the Yser Canal, failed. The number of enemy guns, which we captured to the North of Ypres, has increased to 63.

On the Meuse Heights to the South East of Verdun, our positions were pushed forward some hundred metres.

In the East, the village of Kawale and a Hill to the South, taken. A Russian *point d'appui* captured at Dachowo. A Russian night attack against our positions in the Opor valley repulsed.

April 30.

In Flanders, the bridge-heads at Steenstraate and Het Sas are firmly held by our troops. In the Champagne, the position which we captured to the North of Mesnil consolidated and maintained by our troops against enemy attacks, as well as all other captured positions in the West. The entire losses of the French sustained during the fighting on the Meuse Heights from 24th—28th April amount to 43 officers and 4,000 men.

In Russia, our advanced troops have reached the railway line Dünaburg–Libau on a broad front. Russian attacks collapsed at Kalwarja, suffering heavy losses. Renewed violent night attacks repulsed by our Allied in the Orawa and Opor valley.

From the air war. The coast defence Harwich, on the English East Coast, supplied with German bombs.

German Soldiers' Letters
published in the press by the soldiers' parents and relations

1. From the Western Theatre of War.

The Bath-Train on the Battlefield.

Dear Karl

I hope you got my last letters with all news. To-day I will tell you of something, of which I am sure you have not already heard.

The bath-train is one of the newest of the many admirable arrangements, which the army administration has made for the comfort of our warriors. One of these trains arrived for the first time at the theatre of operations of the... army and caused general admiration and excitement among the troops. The Director of this train is a compatriot of ours, the wellknown scientist and archæological Director from Württemberg, Professor Goessler; the inventor and builder of this moveable bathing institute is also a Swabian, Engineer Zimmermann from Nurtingen. Latter, who is in a field telegraph section, improvised the train in four weeks, assisted by six men, who had been at the front, and in spite of this short space of time, brought it to such perfection, as is proved by the number of shower baths that can be had in one day (900). You will understand that I cannot explain all the different useful and technical arrangements. Besides the shower baths, there is a space allotted for warm baths with hot and cold showers for officers.

The train consists of a Belgian locomotive, which has been characteristically named "Nixe" (Nymph), an 18 cbm. water tank carriage, taken from a French distillery, three Belgian goods carriages, which have been transformed into so many clean shower compartments, and a passengers carriage, which serves as a dressing room with separate compartments. Finally the service carriage, which offers a warlike and modest abode for the professor and engineer, as well as their attendants. The whole train is heated throughout by steam.

The commander of the place had hardly communicated the arrival of the "Nixe" and her suite to the troops, who were enjoying two days' rest here from the trenches, or lying in readiness, when the first troop of bathers started to take advantage of the situation. Our Archæologist has the men advance in two rows, divides them into groups according to the space in the dressing rooms and after a few minutes about 45 very fieldgrey "Adams"

hop into the shower carriages, which are coupled something like a.
D-Zug (Corridor train). The intervening spaces are nicely screened
off. The men take their places under the showers, which are arranged
in double rows, and just have time to admire the clean white enamel
of the walls and ceiling and the clean wooden grating under their
feet, when the bath attendant gives the mechanic a sign by pressing
an electric bell. Water of a temperature of 38° now flows freely
for one minute, after which it is turned off for 2 minutes, during
which the process of soaping is gone through, and at the end the
shower is turned on for three minutes, not without many a merry,
and now and then strong expression being heard. The single phases
of the bathing have been tried and found sufficient; in three days
2,500 men could be freed from their winter crust contracted in the
intrenchments.

How much this arrangement is appreciated, can be seen by the
contented grins on many a bearded warrior's countenance, or ex-
pressions such as: "That was the best of the whole war," or "I
had begun to think that I should have to bring home all the dirt
of the last eight months." Up to this, the troops in the halting
stations (Etappenorte) were the only ones, who could now and
then enjoy a bath; but the bath train fulfills a pressing hygienic
need of the troops in the real front, bringing them comfort, which
is greatly appreciated.

Now the bath train has left for the next station situated at a
distance of 6 kilometres, and already many are looking forward to
its next visit here, which will be in three weeks. Then our professor will again begin his fight against the "Patina," of which he
is a great enemy in warfare; it is only in civil life and in an
archæological direction that he finds the existence of patina justified.

Heartiest greatings from your brother   Fritz.

(Schwäbischer Merkur, March 30, 1915.)

A Captured Copy of the "Morning Post."

My dear parents,

After several hours fighting we took possession of one of the
enemy's entrenchments yesterday, in which I found a "Morning Post"
of 3rd April, lying on the ground, and as soon as we had time, I began to devour its contents. To my great astonishment I came across
an article, which surprised me so much that at first I thought I did
not see aright.

As I suppose that you only see English newspapers rarely or
by chance, I herewith send a translation of the article in question:*

---

* The original copy of "Morning Post" is not at our disposal. Above
is a translation from the German, but as date is given, those interested can
compare with copy 3rd April 1915.

A certain W. F. P. Stockton from Cork, writes to the editor of the "Morning Post":

"On 22nd March, a surgeon wrote to you of men and women that were murdered and referred to the mob and confusion in Munich at the time that war was declared. For anybody, who was in Munich at that time and for many weeks afterwards, this appears to be an absolutely distorted way of dealing, speaking, and thinking . . . Munich was a quiet town last August. The general feeling was that of depression. There was no mob to molest one, because according to our ideas, there was no mob there. All the placards posted up at street corners, whether of victory or defeat, were read quietly. The soldiers and the recruits from the country sang "Volkslieder" (folks songs) when on the march; they were not followed by any crowd. no screaming women were to be seen and there appeared to be no drunken soldiers. Wherever the troops passed by, the women stood still looking after them and thinking of "their poor wives and children."

I speak as a British subject, who had to register at the Police Station, but after the first time was dispensed from reporting, and who had full liberty to wander round —either on foot or with the railway—among the hills of Oberammergau and at that time all British subjects enjoyed the same amount of liberty. Nobody was interned, nor molested, as far as I know, not even criticized. Whoever wishes to know the truth for the sake of unfortunate Europe or from higher and holier interests, need but write to the British Chaplain, who was or is in Munich, or to the American Chaplain, or any of the well-known Americans there, or to a celebrated French scientist, whose name I can give. He continues his studies peacefully in the Munich libraries.

I could even give the names of at least half a dozen Anglo-Bavarians, some of whom considered England's Declaration of War on Germany as wrong, and others, who were heart and soul with England. No matter what their political ideas, all will express their astonishment at persons, who, carried away by passion or rage, or in vulgar thoughtlessness and want of judgment, express sentiments, which make this poor world still poorer and shame us all."

The above extract is reasonable and creditible and it is a pleasure to know that there are still some decent people among the English, who are not afraid of owning to the truth. I am quite well on the whole. The enemy constantly attacks, but without success. On the contrary: Our counter-attacks have been very successful. Let us hope that there will soon be peace and we shall all see each other happy again.

As ever your devoted son
Karl.

The Bhnd Shell.

Erich Oesterheld in the "Berliner Tageblatt" describes an interesting war episode, from which we take the following:

The troops returned to their billets in the village after a small skirmish. About 12 men are in the room of a one-storied house. It is still too early for sleep and the next day is free. So the men sit round the table, telling each other stories over their pipes and try to warm themselves with hot drinks. The room is meagerly lighted by a petroleum lamp. They make a fire in the iron stove that is set in the corner, and very soon the room is warm, cosy and full of tobacco smoke. The thunder of the cannons resounds from a distance, resembling the asthmatic sounds of an enormous hautboy. The men are gay and glad to be in warm shelter, and their humour improves with every minute. Suddenly, in the midst of the warriors' laughter, an almost antediluvian din arises. The men jump up alarmed. It seems as if all the beams were bursting and not a stone of the house could remain in its place. The next moment the ceiling opens and a grenade whizzes into the room. An enormous beam is hanging and swings threateningly above their heads. Dead silence reigns—the laughter and chatter have been stilled as if by magic. Then confused and horrified the screams of the soldiers, some of whom have been slightly wounded, can be heard: "Take care!" .... "grenades!" .... All around is smoke and dust, and everyone rushes to the door. A sergeant, who in his confusion had taken hold of the lamp, stands at the half barricaded door, as the last. These few seconds had seemed to him like eternity. Not far from him under the swinging beam, the grenade had fallen. He stares at it .... now, now, now ..
he hears noise and screaming as if from afar, and in the next moment feels a tug at his arm and is dragged out. For a long time he remained standing, completely dazed, among his comrades, who are all astonished that they are still alive. The shell will not explode. "That was a blind shell" somebody says in a weak voice. "This time we had a lucky escape!" Then they stood silently and pressed each others hands. They all felt that death had been among them, and it seemed as though its shadow still haunted them.

(Süddeutsche Zeitung, March 28, 1915.)

In the Witches' Cauldron.

In an intrenchment, near Reims,
the "Witches' Cauldron," 25. 2. 15.

My dear German Boys,
That was on 15th September.
For 36 hours, the French had threatened our brave Landwehr. Five times they attacked the entrenchments—and five times the attack collapsed under our fire, like the waves breaking against

the rocks. The ground in front was covered with corpses and whereever our splendid machine guns could shoot, there the red breeches lay, whole rows mown down. I counted 28 dead myself at one spot.

The evening of the second day of battle came on. Thank God! For it announced the approach of night, which meant a few hours rest. Hark!—the shooting grows louder and louder. The bullets fall in thousands, like a violent shower of hail, accompanied by shells and shrapnells. '

A fighting ordonnance comes out of the entrenchment, his helmet is on the back of his head, and with the back of his hand he wipes the sweat from his brow.

"Brigadeführer?"

"Here!"

"A report from the left section, the French are again attacking and the Major requests reinforcements, as we have suffered enormous losses."

The General nods assent. A moment later, two companies proceed to the support. We sit there in silence, all around us the noise of Hell. The grenades whizz into the wood. The slope under cover of which the reserves are lying, at least provides some shelter. There—fire—smoke—filth—a dreadful din—we are almost deafened. A shell has exploded at about 20 steps from us. Groans! It has hit the dressing tent. Poor fellows! As I said before, it is like Hell. The "Witches' Cauldron" was the name, which we gave the glen later on. I sit beside my Brigadier General, Exzellenz Graf Vitzthum. Neither of us speaks a word, the bursting of the grenades makes all speech impossible, the earth trembles, and we have a humming in our ears. Again an ordonnance appears: "The enemy has advanced to within 300 metres, the right section asks for reinforcements."

Exzellenz nods again. Two companies—the last. If they cannot fill up the gap, then we are lost.

"Heidemarck?"

"Exzellenz!"

"Ride over to the division! Say that I want the battalion that they have at their disposition, to march here. Tell them of our plight! God be with you." In silence we shake hands. Below my horse is standing quite ready, my faithful servant wants to accompany me. Nobody is to come with me; straight across the fields, of which the enemy commanded a full view? No! Then a small circuit through the wood.

In the meantime I had come full under the shower of bullets. Goodness, how they whizz and hum! Tjuh! Tjuh! Here a branch has been shot off. Tjuh—tac! Now a trunk is hit, so that the bark splashes about like water.

But the red breeches over beyond aim badly, very badly, the bullets prove this. They are meant for our rifles in front, and it is here they fall. Prrrt! Another one has just past my ear. A keyholer, these rebounders are the worst! They cause wounds so large, that you can put your hand in. D...! Now it grows better. Shrapnells! Hui—i—i! The bullets and little lead balls fall on the sand to the right and left of me, one even hitting me in the back—but it falls down without any effect. the explosive was, luckily for me. too high. I continue through the wood, and when the trees get thicker and higher, put the spurs to my horse and start off at a full gallop. My black mare knows what depends on her speed and goes for all she is worth. I have to keep bent so that the branches do not drag off my helmet. In a few minutes I have arrived at an open space, and as I turn in my saddle, can see our position with the pretty clouds of silver, caused by exploding shrapnells and the dust and mud blown into the air by the bursting grenades. And behind the French entrenchments the glow of burning villages and farms. The whole horizon is red.

I proceed, and again come into the wood, which after a few minutes, again grows thin. I can see the hill behind which the village is situated, where the reserves are. I start to gallop again and that was my salvation.

Five Frenchmen block my way with pointed rifles: *"Halte, Qui vive?"*

I give my mare the whip and scream at the patrol:

"En avant! En avant! Mille tonnerres!"

And—imagine, the fellows are taken in. I have come through, hurrah!

The corporal comes after me screaming: *"Hein? Pas compris!"*

I turn a little in the saddle and laughing gaily call out once more: *"En avant! En avant! Mart de ma vie!"* They then set down their guns as they did not quite understand the situation. Owing to the twilight, they could not distinguish my uniform and then the whole affair was over in the twinkling of an eye. I laughed for joy that my ruse had succeeded and proceeded on my errand.

But then I saw a wire fence just before me, more than a metre high, the edges of the field are fenced in with same to prevent the rabbits doing too much damage.

Jump?—Too late! My animal rushes against this at full gallop —and, as if by a miracle, clears it, landing on her knees—but a chuck at the bridle puts her on her feet again.

Hurrah! Now the way leads through brushwood and young birches, the twigs brush against my face and hands, but in a few minutes I reach the high road and see my goal, the village, lying before me. I can hardly bring my mare to gallop again, but at last I reach the first houses—at a short distance the triangular Division's pennon is flying—I slip from my horse, throwing the reins to one of the outposts ..... and two minutes later, the reserves were on the march.

We kept our position, and as a reward for having brought up the battalion in time, I was decorated with the Iron Cross. Boys, just think how proud I am! One of the first six in the brigade to get it. I had to ride a patrol one day, and on my return found the Iron Cross awaiting me. You can fancy how glad I was.

(Rudolstädter Zeitung, March 29, 1915.)

Neuve-Chapelle.

One of the participants in the fighting at Neuve-Chapelle 10th to 13th March, writes the following:

Some Indians, who had come over to us a few days before, made statements as to the possibility of an English attack. It is remarkable that they did not employ any Indian troops this time for the assault itself. Perhaps it was only a trick of the English that they allowed the 25 Indians to come over, so as to lead us astray as to their real intentions. On 10th March, at 8·30 a. m. a fearful cannonade was suddenly set up by about 250 or 300 guns, the noise and din being worse than anything, which I had experienced during the whole campaign. The earth appeared to heave and it was as if hell had broken loose. It was impossible to distinguish the difference between the firing off or the explosion of shells All that one heard was the mighty, hideous, burst of noise, which always seemed to increase.

After a short time, the positions of our . . . battalion and that of the adjacent rifle battalion were but a heap of ruins, it was impossible to think of any defence, as no reserves could be brought up, as all paths, hedges, and houses were covered by the enemy fire. The English kept up this enormous gun fire during the whole day, it being most violent until 11·30 a. m. It would not be over-estimating the number of shots fired off by the English during these three mornings at 40,000 to 50,000, without including the ammunition used by them during the afternoon. It is worthy of attention that these showers of grenades and shrapnells partly from heavy ship guns, were principally directed towards the section held by the two above named battalions, which held the foremost positions. It is correct, that Neuve-Chapelle, which we had taken on 26th October, had to be partly evacuated. But only the foremost trenches, to a depth of two kilometres. That was the success, which the English regulars achieved but only at a very high price, as they were almost decimated by our troops. We have read the Anglo-French "official" reports of Neuve-Chapelle and shaken with laughter at their official lies. Our official report of the fighting at Neuve-Chapelle is absolutely correct. These poor French, how astonished they will be, when they learn the whole truth!

(Stadtanzeiger der Kölnischen Zeitung, April 13, 1915.)

Bavarian Heroism.

(A Company Leader's Report.)

After several days bitter fighting, our brigade had succeeded in clearing the valley of S . . . as far as M . . . . of the enemy, but they still held the frontier pass between French and German Alsace.

Deep, well-fortified trenches straggle along the whole mountain ridge, while enemy batteries are hidden in well-chosen positions, ready to do their murderous work. The French consider their positions impregnable. But our brave Bavarians do not know this word. Under the burning August sun they advance with incomparable and reckless courage against the heights. A French captain said to me afterwards in fluent German: "If I had such soldiers as you, in my position, you would never have come up." And I quite believe him, for each of our brave fieldgreys is a hero. Even if great deeds cannot be done by each one individually, still, we have changed our opinions long ago as to the fact that the single unit is not noticeable in these days of massed armies.

During the course of this war, I have been witness of deeds, carried out with such courage and heroism by simple Reserve and Landwehr-men, who have left wives and children at home—deeds, I repeat, which deserve to be graven in golden letters in the book of history. And whenever I recall the 24th August, the day on which we stormed the Pass, I remember the gallant Reserve-man of the I. Company of our Battalion, Jakob Zimmermann from Nürnberg, Leyherstraße 145, who alone, at a distance of 80 m. from the French trenches, with four of his comrades lying dead around him, offered brave resistance to the enemy. The thicket of the wood, which would have afforded some shelter, was in the rear, but his position was behind a little heap of earth, which afforded but small cover, about a hundred meters off the left wing of his Company. From my position I could observe clearly, how the French took him to task. But what did that matter to him? Should he hurry back to the thicket? Not likely! His Company is to advance and storm the height! And bullet for bullet, each of them well-aimed, is sent across to the enemy trenches.

Suddenly I noticed that the brave fellow turned from the enemy stationed opposite him, and took aim at a wood, which was situated a little to the left. A French officer with 60 men had proceeded from this place to occupy a trench which had been prepared and commanded our left flank. No sooner had I grasped the danger, which threatened our Company, than I see the French leader, hit by one of our brave comrade's bullets, sink to the ground. Most of the French turn tail, only a few of them advance without a leader towards the position. From there they open a violent quick fire at close range on the solitary Bavarian. He answers with a few bullets, but cannot hold out long under such fire. I see his head fall to earth, just as I advance to the assault with our battalion. As soon as we had taken the enemy positions on the whole line, and sent a few rounds of lead after the fleeing French, I went to see what had become of the brave fellow, who had saved our left flank. I found him lying unconscious with a shattered arm, the red blood flowing. copiously from his hips and thighs.

When he regained consciousness that evening in the ambulance hospital at M . . . . ., his wounds had been carefully bandaged; but medical science could not save his arm, it had to be amputated. Not long ago I met this hero in the garrison, decorated with the Gold Medal for Bravery. I asked after his health and endeavoured to comfort him for the loss of his arm. But with brightly beaming eyes he replied: "I did not mind losing it for my fatherland, and if I cannot follow my calling anymore, there will surely be some nobleminded person, who will find occupation for us poor disabled soldiers." *(Casseler Tageblatt, April 21, 1915.)*

2. From the Eastern Theatre of War.

The Shelling of Ossowiec.

The "Königsberger Hartungsche Zeitung" publishes the following letter, which an artillery officer has written to his parents in Königsberg:

It is really revolting and almost incredible, how the Russian General Staff Reports lie. They do not only distort facts, but invent most of them. I do not doubt that the French and English reports are the same. But of course it is quite clear that we cannot officially contradict every silly statement. In that case the reports of our Army Administration would be four times as long as they are at present. Recently we read: "At Ossowiec the enemy brought up some batteries nearer to the fortress after having recognized the fruitlessness of shelling at long range." The truth of the matter is, that a few batteries changed their positions forwards, especially one of them did considerable damage to barracks that are situated about four kilometres behind the position, while hamlets situated at a further distance, have also been subjected to fire. The fortress itself had got its share beforehand. Is this according to Russian ideas a "fruitless shelling," when the central works have been hit so often that for three days fire has broken out at different places, which burnt from morning to evening? Or if for instance another fort is nothing more than a heap of ruins? This is described as "a column that was shelled." Absolute lies! Columns do not come up except under cover of darkness, or if it is absolutely necessary during a battle that they come up behind the artillery.

"Fighting at medium range was continued on 13th and 14th, until night fell, the artillery gaining great advantages."

Where do they know that from? They have seen nothing. And the advantages exist purely in the imagination. How can it be otherwise when they strew the whole ground indiscriminately? I could almost say that on this day we did not lose a man on the whole line before the fortress, to say nothing of the artillery.

"Two companies of Germans tried to approach the frozen Bobr by way of the village of Goniondz, but had to retire suffering heavy losses."

It is regrettable that I must here repeat: "Absolute lies!" It is possible that some foreposts or patrols advanced a little further in this direction, but that, which the Russian report states, is not true.

"In the vicinity of Ossowiec, our spies discovered some enemy posts and brought them as prisoners to the fortress.

The cutting off of listening posts, which occurs now and then, is not an event worthy of being mentioned in a General Staff Report. In another report it is stated that a fleet of airships had flown over the fortress, dropping hundreds of bombs. Again absolute lies! The new commander of the fortress appears to wish to give Nikolajewitsch the impression, that his post is a particularly difficult one and in this way earn all the more praise for his endurance.

(Berliner Lokalanzeiger, April 10, 1915.)

Fighting at close Quarters.

A volunteer from Cassel, who was severely wounded in one of the battles in Russia, very soon after having gone to the front, describes his experiences in a letter from a hospital in Johannesburg (East Prussia) in the following manner:

... After some bitterly cold days and still worse nights we arrived absolutely worn out on the evening of 13th March in L...., having marched 42 kilometres across impossible roads. In the "Salon" of a remarkably filthy peddler's house, which was burnt down by a Russian shell eight days later, 23 of us rested on straw, while in the kitchen, which was next door, the Polish family of 12 were packed still tighter together. It was Sunday, the 14th March, Divine Service was held in the pretty pale-blue wooden church, flanked on each side with two turrets, after which we marched off to the entrenchments. Latter extend 10—15 m. from the edge of the opposite wood, parallel with the Russian trenches, that are situated at about 400—1,000 m. distance from a bog, which is partly frozen. Dug-in in loose, yellow sand there are no difficulties about cleaning rifles and after some time one grows accustomed to the whizz of the Russian bullets. The Russian troops opposed to us here, are Siberian regiments and not to be despised, as their forces are very strong. But our positions are to be held at all costs! Two Russians, who fell into the hands of [a corporal, attached to the field kitchens, who had gone astray, said, that the Russians had planned an attack towards midnight. As leader of the 7th group, which was told off to hold one of the curves in our entrenchment, I had a difficult post; the listening post which was stationed 200 m. in advance of our line in an alder bush. I took over from 1—3 o'clock. A fine rain. sleet and snow accompanied by an icy wind, did not enhance the comfortable place situated as it was, 400 m. from the Russian position. However. the night passed quietly. On the morning of the 15th, our artillery set up a lively fire, and the Russians, that could be seen fleeing from the dug-outs, showed what good work our howitzers had done in the Russian entrenchments. Towards midday the fire ceased, and we leaders of groups were allowed to divide "Liebesgaben" among our men, consisting of sausages, cigars and cigarettes.

Towards evening the weather cleared up, and now a hellish noise was set up by our and the Russian artillery, which increased with the darkness. I sent my men with the exception of one, to sleep in the dug-out, although on this night an attack could be expected. But shortly after midnight, the fire balls and artillery firing died away. The next morning, we were to be relieved, having had 45 hours trench service, but it was midday before we again arrived at L.... Our quarters were occupied, and we were distributed in barns where we could rest. But at 5·30 p.m. we were again collected, as we had to form reserves. This was a nice surprise! We had to dig the snow out of three holes and lying on the frozen ground covered with rugs, partially protected from the snow by pieces of tent canvas, which we had erected, we lay on the alarm, shivering and trembling with cold. We were so uncomfortable that when the alarm was given towards 2·30 a.m., we were almost glad. A nice concert was going on. The Russians had crawled on towards our right wing and taken two German guns. We were to recapture them. The Russian search-lights flashed through the pine trees and a few shrapnells burst over our heads. Then all was pitch dark again. "Swarm out to the left, the road is the right frontier—forwards!" That was the command. A man in my group was slightly wounded in the neck, but the corporal bandaged him up, while 50 steps in front of us, there was a fearful din. The Russians had come into our entrenchments. We could not open fire, as owing to the darkness we would have hit our comrades. The serjeant is shot in the arm. As leader of the group, I advanced a few steps, climbed over a hill and waited for my men. No good, I try to crawl back, but I see the Russians approach, eight men come forward, jabbering words, which were unintelligible. I opened the breech-lock with incomparable speed and fired off five rounds successfully. Four of the Russians stumble, the four others at my back. I could feel the cold blade of a bavonet penetrating about 4 cm. above my right shoulder, some blows with the butt end of guns finished me off. Fresh Russians stormed past and one man hits me in the face with the butt end of his gun. One of the Russians tries to find valuables and takes a three Mark piece out of my purse, the nickel and copper coins he puts back. Luckily for me, he did not find my watch and ring in the darkness. Another gives the impression of wanting to spear me, but mostly the blades are stopped by my ribs. Some more knocks on my helm and head, but at last the Russians have passed. By degrees light dawns, but the blood, which has flowed over my eyes and whole face, prevents my seeing anything. I take good care not to move. Suddenly towards half past five, the Russians begin to flee wildly. I can feel them stumbling and falling over me. At 5·45, the first Germans—about 6 o'clock, one of the ambulance men drags me out of the heap of Russians and carries me to L...., where I was bandaged and remained in the ambulance of the Presbytery until the 24th. .... ⟨*Casseler Allgemeine Zeitung, April 13, 1915.*⟩

3. From the Fleet.

Extract from the letters of the Naval Chaplain on Board the "Gneisenau."

Letters written by the naval chaplain of the "Gneisenau," Pastor Hans Rost, that have now been published in the "Daheim," give a description of the naval battle of Santa Maria, which is imperishable in the history of ⟨the ⟨young German fleet. Two of these letters are as follows:

My dear Parents,

On Friday, the 30th October, at 2 o'clock in the morning, we sighted the lights of Valparaiso for the first time and then returned in the darkness of night to look for the enemy, whom we had heard was off the Chilian Coast. Early on Sunday morning, our wireless got traces of him, but it was only towards 4·15 p. m. that we sighted him. The command had just been given: "Clear the guns for the night!" The same command as was whistled down every afternoon between 4—5·15 p. m., when one of the first officers rushed past my cabin calling out: "Pastor, there is something doing! The English are there!" It was my neighbour at table, Oberleutnant Schwede, with whom I came out just a year ago. He had celebrated his birthday on 30th October, the speaker on this occasion wished him the joy of living to see the great day, and now the momentous instant had arrived. At 4·50 p. m., I went to the principal dressing station, where all kinds of reports were afloat. I asked—for up to this there had been no time to ask—who and what was coming. At first the enemy turned tail, so as to collect—we after him without

knowing exactly, how many ships weie before us, as all that could
be seen was the smoke. At 5·37 p. m. I heard fiom Leutnant K.
that there are four ships before us: "Good Hope," "Monmouth,"
"Glasgow," and "Otranto." From the upper deck I could see at
a distance of about 15 kilometres, parallel with us, line ahead the four
ships—first four, then three, then two or three small ones, and at
last two high funnels (the auxiliary cruiser). At 5·42 p. m. I went
down again and the next moment heard the command: "Fern-
gefecht an Steuerbord!" In thc meantime it is 6·36 p. m. when the
fiist shots are heard. At 10 minutes past 8 o'clock, I went to my
cabin to see whether it is still there. A lamp shade is cracked, a
water pitcher has turned over, as well as my alarm clock, but latter
is still going and the hands point to 8·10 p. m., that was all. With
a grateful heart I laid myself to rest shortly after 11 o'clock.
Greetings from   Hans.

                                        Off Valparaiso, 3. 11. 14.

On Sunday, 1st November, we had a political Reformation
feast. 6·26 p. m. until 8 o'clock, a fight between "Schainhorst,"
"Gneisenau," "Leipzig" and "Nürnberg" against "Good Hope,"
"Monmouth," "Glasgow" and an English auxiliary cruiser. The
laige cruiser "Monmouth" sunk, "Good Hope" disappeared in the
darkness on fire, "Glasgow" escaped.—We had no one killed!'
"Gneisenau" had two wounded to report. What an achievement
after thiee months impatient waiting! In the morning I had taken
foi the text of my sermon Ebr. 13,9: "Es ist ein köstlich Ding, daß
das Herz fest werde, welches geschieht durch Gnade."

Love to you all from   Hans.

The gallant naval chaplain who wrote above, has lost his life
since. A few days later, at the battle of the Falkland Islands he
was severely wounded, while looking after the injured and went
down with the "Gneisenau."

                                  (Fränkischer Kurier, March 21, 1915.)

4. From the Air Fleet.

A Fight in the Air with French Aviators.

                                        Cambrai, April 6, 1915.

Latterly, we airmen noticed a great deal of railway traffic
behind the French positions, and so Leutnant d. R. G...., who,
as a young observer, was to make his first flight over the enemy
positions, and I, got orders to advance on a flight to A...., which
is about 120 kilometres distance from Cambrai, and to make re-
reconnoissance notes of the whole territory. On leaving our posi-

tions, I ascended to a height of about 2,000 metres, and on approaching A.... flew over the enemy lines, so as to arrive at our goal along the main-road and railway line route. On the way, my observer generously supplied an enemy battery, which had made itself very noticeable, with a small-sized bomb. A short time after, when we saw our goal in the distance, owing to the clear weather, we met a German biplane followed by a French monoplane, both machines flying about 800 metres higher than we were. My observer did not take my advice, which had been to take aim at the monoplane with his carbine.

We flew on, and after a few minutes met a French Farman-biplane, with whom we resolved to have a fight. But just at the moment that I had turned to the right at a sharp angle, so as to afford my observer better aim, I heard a report just behind me and received two violent blows on the head, which robbed me of consciousness for a couple of seconds—but luckily, only for a couple of seconds. When I had myself and my machine again in hand, I could feel my blood warmly trickling down my head and at this moment, just as formerly in my student days at a "Mensur," I boiled with rage. I tugged at my machine, which had sunk about 100 metres during my short span of unconsciousness, veering round, and now my observer showed me the little French monoplane, which had flown past us a short time before in pursuit of the other German air machine. At this altitude another Farman-biplane and a second monoplane cut off our way to the rear.

When my observer had taken up the unequal fight with his pistol against the two new opponents, the two first machines reached and opened fire on us. The Farman-biplane had hit my benzin tank and cooling pipes, with its machine gun. We passed through some dreadful minutes, locked in, and under fire from all sides. I dived and curved with my machine, which had received a mortal wound in her most vulnerable part, her benzin heart. I knew, the machine could not hold out much longer, so I darted to the left, to the right, taking all possible directions, and we were still about 15 kilometres from our most advanced trenches, over enemy territory. All kinds of thoughts raced through my brain. Should I try to ram the enemy? Then we would both be brought down. Just at this moment the first French monoplane came up, from which I had received the two shots in my head, it advanced slowly with the propeller directly against us, as if it wished to give us the fatal blow at near range. In a rage that bordered on dispair, I threw my biplane against it, crying out to my observer: "Take care"! and rushed past the Frenchman at a distance of about 5 metres enabling my observer to quickly fire off some shots. They must have been well aimed, for the calm gliding flight of the Frenchman quite suddenly changed to a steep—and turning over, the machine disappeared to the ground. That appeared to have shaken the nerves of the other Frenchmen, for they at once cleared the way for us towards A. . . ., which to my joy I saw lying to oui right. The second monoplane approached us once more, but he probably shared the same fate as his comrades, as after some well-aimed shots sent off. by my observer, he disappeared in a precipitate gliding flight, towards home.

The two Farman-biplanes now began to pursue us, but never came very close, keeping us under fire from their machine. guns till we arrived at the entrenchments. Their fire, however, was not so disagreeable as that of the French artillery, which now began firing at us for all it was worth, as we had come over their positions, and owing to the defect in my motor could not rise higher than 900 metres. The little clouds of shrapnell smoke, which were particularly disagreeable at this altitude, appeared in masses all round. A slight report and flame, and a little cloud, distributed every now and then some fatal pieces of iron. Luckily, we got through the dangerous little objects, sometimes round about, sometimes below or above until finally we arrived behind our own lines, where I was able to land smoothly at our advanced flying base. My observer and I shook each others hands warmly, as we had much cause to be grateful to one another.

The two shots, which I had received from the Frenchmen, had been very well meant. One went through the lining of my helmet and just missed my forehead, but the other took a piece of skin about 10 cm. in length from the middle of my skull laying bare the bone. However these two wounds are healing well, although they will take some time, but I hope soon to be able to make some new flights.   *(Berliner Lokalanzeiger, April 14, 1915.)*

Lightning Source UK Ltd.
Milton Keynes UK
UKOW06f1903270717
306203UK00006B/568/P

9 781330 402979